citizen Of

Citizen Of

Christian Hawkey

WAVE BOOKS SEATTLE • NEW YORK

Published by Wave Books
www.wavepoetry.com

ISBN-13: 978-1-933517-16-2 Trade Paper
ISBN-13: 978-1-933517-17-9 Limited Edition Hardcover

Wave Books titles are distributed to the trade by
Consortium Book Sales and Distribution
1045 Westgate Drive, St. Paul, Minnesota 55114

Library of Congress Cataloging-in-Publication Data:

Hawkey, Christian, 1969-
  Citizen of / Christian Hawkey. — 1st ed.
    p. cm.
  ISBN-13: 978-1-933517-17-9 (alk. paper)
  ISBN-13: 978-1-933517-16-2 (pbk. : alk. paper)
  I. Title.

PS3608.A89C58 2007
811'.54—dc22

2006038910

Designed and composed by J. Johnson
Printed in the United States of America

9 8 7 6 5 4 3 2 1

FIRST EDITION

Wave Books 010

It is moved by us and in those moments when
as if from the nests of names
things break loose in a frenzy, in free fall
(in ascending perceptions? things seen to the side?)

Arkadii Dragomoschenko

CONTENTS

O

O

O

HOUR

There was a lump
in the landscape

tho it had no throat
it spoke to those who

got on their knees
to listen to it

a titmouse
landed & instantly

vomited on it
blowflies

swarmed in &
stuck to it

some thought it was a
hidden camera

& therefore wept
all over it

in this way it
came to be a mound

WATER IN THE EAR

We exchanged looks—all three of us—
& mine was totally better: it had rose-colored sequins
glued along the hemline & the word sneezeweed
in one pocket & an open window
with the sound of cows ripping through spring grass
filtering through it. We were filtering through it.
We were filters. We had to use our tongues to remove
the pollen collecting in the corners of our eyes
which were oversized, slightly joined, lidless.
A squirrel mounted the bottom of a drainpipe
& waited there, expectantly. It was kind of sexual
although Morty observed it was "just a rat
with a beautiful ass; in fact, in the original Latin . . ."
We exchanged looks again & this time
blonde women in gold lamé jumpsuits
handed out birds with brand names
sewn into their breasts. Their beaks
were frozen open. I'd never seen a bird pant.
I threw it up into the air but it
dropped softly to the cement
so I stomped on it—I don't know why—
such is the nature of instinct & the
vertical surge of skyscrapers, porcini mushrooms,
the invisible teeth of lichen, sinking into a stone,
how blushing is one part sincerity, one part stupidity,
the clarity of a line of drool
swinging from an infant's
glossy chin . . . From such a distance

it was hard to tell why he
whacked the side of his head
against the air. We paused, & even the dogs
paused with us, listening.

HOUR

My chest is a kind of topsoil
it always slips off in the rain
it has drawers for every insect
I tuck my head into my sternum
a rapid beak nibbling is the
most efficient form of preening
there are glands in my cheeks
I know nothing of how they work
although I am drawn to rubbing them
against the tips of car antennae
fence posts the end of a big toe
often I bite the skin of my arm
and let go the indent is a circle
of books my skin a shelf
submerged in the air it marks
the border of an island
how happy for the land to have an eye
a string of islands is a beautiful sight
the ocean uses them to spy on us
this puddle just winked at me
Donald doesn't like me anymore
his chest is in my teeth
he reads me to sleep at night when
the wind floats the house out
from under my skin into the stars
eating so many holes
in the island the sky the weather
a sweater falling apart in my hands

REPORT FROM THE UNDERSECRETARY
OF INQUESTS

Gender: indeterminate. Age:
ancient. Eyes: undersized.
Nose: broken. Neck: connected.
Hair: mostly air. Chest: at rest.
Gender: pending. Forehead: dented,
perhaps by stars or star-shaped devices
such as a Phillips head, although
the tongue, twisted, recently located
inside the right cheek
salutes you, clearly
as shadows salute the sun's love
of late afternoons in winter trees
leafless as the word branches.
I'm awake. I'm awake. Minutes
more a few minutes more &
a face the morning twitches into
movement is blinking. Where's
my war bonnet. Birdlessly the sky.
Blue is a hole in my head you
fly into, whispering, questioning.
A cat's feathered tongue. Its patiences.
Spring. Coiled sources. They pulled
the river out of the body
called today, Tuesday,
did you know her wide, flat gaze
& the way it moved

or certain things move, as if
from beneath, unseen the earth, like
a bull's shoulder must flow suddenly sideways
for a fly. Flecknoe
is his name. He lives under the sign
of The Sad Pelicans, which are easy
to find since their leathery,
weather-beaten distensible gular pouches
unfold with a little wind
as gray, overcast skies. & what's with
I lost my thought. You are
a coy mistress. A jade-gray chalcedony
curtains your neck which is long,
& curving, & carries
like a column of flesh-colored liquid
your head through rooms, windows, walls
made of mist, backlit. Can anyone
tell me who Phillips was. Each life
is a tool. We're holding
our own hands. We're turning in slow motion
held together by a few screws,
this wrist, a Tuesday, light
allowing all the patterns
& how they blur into you, as you.

HOUR UTOPIC

Incoming: field strafed by fireflies.
Incoming: sand shelled by enemy waves.
Landmines whisper sideways underground.
A horseshoe crab is a beautiful helmet.
I extend my limbs entirely into the air
& a sleeping flock of pink flamingos
explodes into morning, the sun stained red
behind outstretched wings, dew
burning off my flak jacket of grass.
Let the Age of Evaporation begin:
the mouths of animals have names.
At night the jaws of turtles creak open
to collect rain, heat lightning
reflected in their wide, sad eyes.
A tear falls. A turtle tear! Two musk deer
shiver across a meadow, dusk
a brief firefight, our names
appear & disappear, like that.
Alison I stored in a bottle in the ground.
I'm standing on a love song. I can hear it tick.
I'm standing in a field with one leg tucked up
into my chest, craning my neck around the necks
of birds, their beaks dipped in ink,
a feather wrote the first word, language
came from the sky, a secret whispered
into a hole, the hole shaped like a bottle,
the earth filled with glass, our names

cool into eyes, I hold mine in my hands:
Love song. Evaporation. Let the countdown
begin—pink night eclipsing
a yellow sun, a glass beach
shattered by a chrome-tipped wave,
two glass eyes blown apart
in my hands . . . A head dents the grass.
Three of the holes swirl with strings of mist.

SMALL REPAIRS IN THE SKY

Something over there, murmuring.
An image-stream, lost,
invisible among the dry leaves,
meandering. A book opens.
A hand opens. Satellites
if I am utterly still I hear
your loneliness. We
a race toward concave faces. Swivel
for a second into a map
of a squirrel's brain: everything's
double-checked, & in place.
Something over there, rustling.
Someone's throat swallows
next to me, in me, a painting
of a throat or only throats
extended, their endless, soft work,
their effortlessness (in laughter).
I could spend a life trying to surprise
my cat. Winters
we sew the fallen leaves
of the plum tree
into a wreath & hang it
back among its branches. Instantly
a hand or a hand puppet
if you thread the fingertips
with green. All alphabets
are manual, seasonal. Never in dancing

knew how to get around my bones.
Pull the thread tighter, Hortense.
If things of sight such heavens be
a video of lost footage
recovered in the act of reading
& when you look up, a film
projected on the wall, called Wall,
& the woman in white, hands
trailing green thread
& a purple wreath of leaves around her head
entering, there
where a door should be, an absence,
spliced. If a skywriter, write clouds.
Some words, unless photographed,
never drift apart.

HOUR WITH ONE HAND INSERTED IN A TIME OF WAR

We dug with our hands & hand shovels.
We dug with our spatulate feet.
& with torsos our only circumference
we dug a maze. A maze of passageways:
Level Three the Maternity Ward, April
with knees on either side of her chin.
Some thoughts no wider than a chest.
Some thoughts no wider than a chest,
heaving. On Level Six a green parrot opened
its red beak & it reached us, seconds later,
as a roar. Our eyelashes cringed, & lashed back.
We named it the Level of Roaring Parrots
& turned back to our work, carrying sewage out
by moonlight, the buckets light each night
& getting lighter. A gas lamp flickered
beside a makeshift waterfall. Ceilings
of soil shook soil. Joo plucked her eyebrows
with her eyes closed, a kind of faith. &
from the mouth of an infant a cracked nipple
slipped—what minerals are my lips
or packed vegetation my eyes—black coals—
how darkness changes darknesses each time
I blink, & blink again, Level One's filling
with tear gas, swing through the Level of
Eternal Foliage & seal it off—April you there,
Yes, I'm here, October's on the Level of Yellow Orioles

Warbling High in the Shadowy Summer Woods
& Gungjeong was last on the Level of Indentations
Left Behind by Falling Snow & should we
stand guard at the Level of One Hand Raised
to Block the Lemon Seed of the Sun
or should we push off, down the tunnels,
dig a hole in the side of a wall & wait?

HOUR OF LUCID VEGETATION

Audiovisual sky, crimped
by a skein of geese,
our skeletons locked

upwards & into place.
Look up, & the mouth
drops open. Look up

& the sky drops in
—a blue guest—
one white cloud snagged

on the tip of our
brainstems. Drainage
occurs, in real time.

& the one who told me
our posture determines
our experience of time

was standing over me.
I was lying down. A
water-bead shot

down the weathered surface
of a fence post, which rotted
right before my eyes.

ELKE ALLOWING THE FLOOR TO RISE UP, OVER HER, FACE-UP

Alone in a room with a video camera
means you're not alone, but lonely.
The floor closed around my lips.
I spoke from a knot. All bodies
are flexible, interlace. A forest
sliced into sections & rearranged
on a horizontal plane: go ahead,
walk on me. I have a wind-up windpipe
vulcanized by the luggage I
arrived with, which is nothing,
nothing special. Swab
my armpits for explosives.
I was never decked out in hairlessness.
The Queen of Spades has the deepest grave.
In the security chute where all passengers
are X-rayed—blue liver, red heart,
white bones—I did a little dance.
I was taken aside. It was a random check.
Yes, by strangers I have received
these hands, unclaimed, these eyes,
unmonitored, these lips
with no return address
in speaking. & those who are shy
would never commit suicide with a gun
because the sound alone
would kill them. Let's

get a peacock on the squawk box.
Let's oscillate between
ocelots, one spot at a time.
You can strap a camcorder on the back
of a humpback & all one sees,
at a certain depth, are stars
& beyond the stars, a green, fluorescent mud,
& beneath the mud
a handful of bones, the bones
of a right hand
clutching a flag, the first flag
ever recorded, the flag of the Elamites, from Elam,
whose language remains indecipherable
& whose flag, significantly,
was too small to ever wave
& therefore only waved in private, in praise.

HOUR

Out of what perhaps need I
take my place among the manufactured
willow trees weeping in a thousand directions
passing on our left the Project of Collecting
Clouds is underway which way to the
Engine Room the Personality Room
the Room of Automatic Misting Systems
Landfills and Instant Refills let the belt
carry you to the Pleasure Chute
the Sadness Chute the Chute Designed
to Make One Feel at Home on the way to
intermittent bursts of flames from smokestacks
(map a city whatever way you can)
such a beautifully run factory you have it
makes my lungs drift together
through the slats I could almost inhale
an infant cloud a cloud untrained in
thunder my eyes two water-beads
jostled together on a leaf the Project
of Recycling Monads is this way
move quickly the trick is to
avoid returning with the need you
began with the desire to surrender
slightly offscreen it's nice for a sec
to wait here alongside you
how long will this last as long as

we're both riding in the same direction
a grove of willow trees leaning in a wind
leaning to the left the light always leans
in both directions against us in this way
we are happily held vertically alive

THE PERFORMING UNDERSTANDING

She with gunpowder draws
an outline of her body
on the grass
& lights it, ignites one end of it,
lays down she her body
inside of it, a charred imprint,
her body, smoking, she
whose figure unravels with wind
as a signal, its movement, smoke
lifting as the grass turns the color
of her hair, black, coal black, burned.
A rooster, nearby, cocks his head.
A fat man, farther away, considers
the phrase "fat chance." & on the shore
of an unnamed shore
he with his body as log or oarfish
rolls away from the waves as they
arrive, now rolls toward them
as they pull away, erasing, erasing,
the one song the waves know,
or the sand knows, if they sang,
which they don't. Someone at some point
picks up a camera. Someone
at some point always does. But before
this the man whose mind
was cold & concentrated on the shape
of a waterlogged log

was simply rolling, back & forth,
with the waves, with himself, singing,
since his mouth in one image is in my mind
open. All of us stepping around
each moment as if it were a snapshot,
a film still, lost footage, footing.
Offscreen, the rooster unrolls
a long yellow ribbon of sound from his beak.
It is spring. No one's around.
White dandelions
bloom the shape of a woman's body.
With a little wind, she moves—migrates.

HOUR

I was lying on my side, in a ditch,
soaking my flanks in bog water
with my head propped up, on an elbow,
highway a few inches from my nose.
Semis thundered past. The grass
flattened its ears. My body shook.
I was humming a song. This was my spot.
Tadpoles are a form of punctuation.
Frogs hide inside commas. A whooping crane
landed & began showing off its legs.
Birds go for the eyes, I thought,
so I looked away, humming a song
about looking away, about looking back,
about fingers wrapped around the flesh
that holds the ribs down to the hips
& hot mangoes rotting, the ground littered
with yellow suns, drainpipe
where the field ends, its dark ooze
the greenest earth. A man walks by
with a giant crucifix on his back
—ALASKA BY SPRING!—cars
speed up to pass him, which makes sense,
even the whooping crane leaves without a sound.
My jaw is wired shut. I'm humming a song
about cleaving, the body drifting apart & what
keeps us from dissolving at the first
drop of rain, my left flank almost

marinated, a sprig of rosemary between my lips,
robots have been dispatched to remove me,
all fruit mirrors the sun, a black seed
against my heart, a black car
driving past, buffeting my chest
& a cell phone lands, right in front of my face:
"It's alright," I whisper into it, "a French donkey,
called a Poitou, whose long ropes of fur
drag along the ground,
was also used, in the mid-to-late 18th century, to polish floors."

HOUR

There were three of us—not sure—
I & I & I, maybe more.
A fuzzy, caterpillary light
crawled across our breastplates
& pigeons—we were in a city—milled
around our ankles, working their
cashew beaks, their perfectly circular
skulls, their clockwork feet
before needing to be wound again
& set free. You wanted to leave
but I wouldn't let you—pardon my shoulders,
they shake when I laugh,
the way the tip of a ship's mast
records, for no one—not even the sky—
the contours of a given wave
—shut up Tony, those were my best days,
wind-swept sea-flashes, brief glitter of glitter
& gently, to prevent injury, I fall to my
kneepads, fully prepared
to pray—is there another way?
A blue goat draws a blue cart
across a meadow, Jimmy at the reins
& Lucy with her hands thrown high overhead
& Tony—are you there Tony—forget Tony—
Jimmy's fallen asleep somewhere in the back
& Lucy is alone counting the stars
in the holes on the bottom of her bunk

& this was the first miracle, talking
to her eyes until they blinked
one by one awake to take in the day
& then at night, they were taken out
& set aside, on the nightstand, where they slept,
rolling sometimes to the right,
a little to the left, never to the floor.

BENEFIT

I was on mute. When it came time. Applause
a wall of carbonated
sound. Then a white mule
was led onto the stage; its nose
leaned into the mic and spoke the words
"Mutual Fund." More applause. "If I stand up
too fast," the mule added, then collapsed. In the wings
the Dalai Lama gathered his robes and exploded.

HOUR OF A MOUTH PACKED WITH FLOWERS

and heated into glass. I put my lips to the wall and blow a window
and my eyes take for themselves what they need, a blue triangle, sky.
I hang it inside. Lying there with sand in my mouth
I tell myself it's only a lie, which is better than telling the others
about a sky. There are no "others."
My lungs don't like this. Neither does the Emperor. He wants his robes,
he wants his little hat back, the one that makes his eyes bulge.
Sometimes when he falls asleep at the throne I remove the pillow
from under his feet. His legs dangle & we all laugh, coughing quietly.
& when a fleck of saliva makes its way
to the corner of his mouth I resist
lifting it off; a province
could disappear, struck down by drought, it's that easy. O where
in these kingdoms red with the clay of sunsets
pasted onto our brows
& these wires threaded with copper
listening to our every desire as if it were a need
can I rest with my blue triangle and maybe, if the light is right,
place my heart inside it, a soft cloud. The sky unspools over
    these borders
like a two-ply roll
of toilet paper; who pointed
my genitals toward the rising sun? And why this
stone set in my chest,
cavity I cannot reach to breathe upon, or polish?

HOUR

From high shelves I took down
laughter without a sound it was late
faces opening on the television
dew collecting on the small hands
of squirrels some creatures move
a few inches every time they blink
I opened my eyes you were my wife
hand a little lower on my spine
although always the smell of tires
burning through the night some creatures
move a few inches each time they flinch
these are the hardest to shake hands with
if you walk slow enough people will
stare at you give you money perhaps weep
we scattered at the first sign of rain
but Strom simply stood there
water gushing from the holes in his shoes
I would like to be a drainpipe
any way to serve the rain
imagine a squirrel wrapping its hands & feet
around your neck some people
are made entirely of neck-matter
yellow cones used to divide highways
& the beauty of Parmigianino is that he painted
the Madonna from the perspective of the infant
Christ sucking on a breast looking up
at the high tower rising to a little shelf
where the face sits the one with a smile
that fits perfectly across her mouth like a label

WHILE YOU WERE OUT

I was here, inhabiting a room
& within the room I had
another room—my head—more empty
than the room I was in, since I
was in it, along with my cat,
who doesn't believe in rooms
or closed rooms, doors.
I don't either. But a door
was there & a door without a room
isn't a door but a gate. It was a gate.
It had a hinge. It had two hinges.
It squeaked like a gate should squeak
when I opened it. It opened. It was a gate.
I was hungry for it to transform me,
moving through it, but it didn't,
it just opened, & so I sat down
within it, holding either side of it
& it didn't seem to mind it.

TREATISE ON THE ELASTIC SKIN OF SURFACES

When I touched you
you crumbled

into a mound
of soft, cold bees. There

was a hole in the roof.
There was no roof.

I saw something flit
between two stars.

There were no stars.
I saw suddenly projected

on the back of my hand
your face, but when I

raised it the light
flicked off & I was left

in the dark with my hand,
my own hand, pressed

against my lips. Very clever,
I whispered, knowing

you were near. Something
moved in a painting

on the wall across from me.
I drew close.

It was a photograph.
I drew closer.

It was a surveillance monitor.
I saw you in a blonde wig

moving down aisle 9.
I saw you step into an elevator

& look me right in the eye.
I saw the back of you recede

down a long, badly lit corridor.
I saw you enter a room

& slowly, methodically,
as if following instructions,

undress. I saw you in a waiting room,
in a dressing room,

incognito, in a cage.
I saw you flit between two cars.

You were a slip
of paper, something

tiny & torn off
lifted by the wind down an alley,

over a balcony, a rooftop.
In the aerial cam you were

the one expressionless face
in the stadium, the one person

looking away, eyes closed,
taking in the sound of people

screaming, cheering, a wall
of orange noise

one inch from your cheek.
Something grazed

the back of my neck. I rotated
inside a meadow

with green dragonflies
suspended in the air

around me, motionless,
a black goat's cud

frozen in the moment of
sideways chewing

& then everything moved,
you moved, were moving

toward me in the tall grass
(sound of feet parting long blades)

& then you skipped, your image skipped
& jumped back, the dragonflies

reset themselves, the screen
flickered once & started over:

I was stumbling backwards
pushed by the wind traveling out

ahead of you, by some far-off
rising applause until I

fell back, waving, into an elevator
which, when the doors closed,

began to move sideways.

O

For from the moment you left,
Like the Hare crouched in its seat
I strain my ear, hearing muffled steps,
Baffled by the darkness over Egypt.

Maurice Scève

BIRTH OF A NATION

"We are witnessing the birth of a nation."
                —NPR journalist on the inauguration of
                East Timor, 19 May 2002

Did the world squat down & push out
a nation? Was it a nation before the world
called it a nation? Do they have customs?
Do they honor the power cats have over ice?
Is their nation-birthing being observed? Hello, I'm Hans.
Do they have a way of identifying their citizens?
Do they brand them? Give them a number?
Are they immune to certain diseases?
Are pharmaceutical operatives surreptitiously
lifting during the night skin samples from their shins?
Will they have a military to defend their borders?
Perhaps they are an island. Can they defend
themselves against the sea? Are their children
born with missing limbs, heads fused to armpits?
Do they consider such children Gods? Heads of state?
Beings who are born into pain and, as a result,
capable of sensing rogue cellular structures
from great distances, capable of dreaming
their way into a perfect world, capable of
feeling the future of an entire nation
in a phantom limb? Do they have
a national language? If someone says "crustacean"
will another think "well-armored vehicle"?

If someone says "soda jerk" will another think of a
large, possibly obese child
attacking a coke machine with a crowbar?
If someone says "spirit" will another start
choking, uncontrollably, to his death?
Do they speak in clicks & soft exploding accents?
Do they sound, at large gatherings, like a popcorn machine?
Do they communicate with their strangely powerful shoulders?
Do they articulate panic by squeezing air
through their tear ducts? Does this cleanse
the national language? Is it on the brink
of extinction? Is a dead language a body
that has consumed itself
to the point of having no point? Is a dead language
any empty stomach, growling? Is a dead language
capable of speaking beyond its own grave, late at night,
when a low moon drifts
through the banyan roots and a child wakes,
unable to wake, and begins whispering for the sake of
whispering, for the sake of keeping time with his pulse?
Do they incinerate their dead? Do they make soap from the ashes?
Is cleanliness a way of honoring the dead? Do they,
as a nation, have a genetic weakness
for alcohol? Are they predisposed to sudden defecation?
And is the measure of a nation how they dispose
of their waste? (If an island, how sad for the sea.)
Do they have a flag? Is it a thumbnail, a painted tooth, a tattoo
on the eyelid so that, at night, the nation sleeps
as one nation? And the colors? Lampblack
to celebrate their powers of night vision? Peach, for sensuality.
Neon mahogany to symbolize their love of wood products?

Would other nations refuse to fly such an ugly flag?
Do their children reach 300 lbs before the age of eight?
What is their relationship to pornography?
If it were declared a national holiday
would it be a more productive nation? Do they flay
their grapefruits section by section
or do they surrender to a total mess?
Do they teach their children the delicacy of inhaling
low-flying clouds? Do they worship herons, or long
to break their legs? Do they worship, upon waking,
the first object they see—even if it's themselves—
or do they move through the day as if it were another day,
not the one they're living, the one with cars
shining quietly in parking lots, an infant sleeping
in a chrome shopping cart, a man hurling
his cell phone against a brick wall
and the clouds opening up, draining the sky blue,
starlings unwrapping a sycamore tree,
the long migrations about to begin?

HOUR

My sixth sensurround
is down, my second skin
the skin I'm stepping
into: I lick
a new finger & hold it up
to the wind: O my beloved
what. O
my beloved what. O my
beloved star-nosed mole
can I clean the soil
from your black, sightless eyes
can I massage with fine oils
your tiny, webbed feet
are you tired of running
into drainpipes
does your mouth foam
approaching power lines
are your tunnels collapsing
do you have work to do
does the dirt breathe
do you breathe the air
between the dirt
are your lungs
the size of earlobes
do you hear me
in the tunnel next to you
have you cut your nose

on a shard of glass
have you excavated
the severed, blue leg
of Spiderman
did you pause to admire
his red booties
are your tunnels collapsing
do you have work to do
am I keeping you
am I keeping you

BLUE YODEL #1

Sewn inside a left hip a highway
paved with the blue tongues of coyotes
a song a blue song
I am far from
the sound of your pupils

a shower curtain the color
of your body behind it I
remember a candy that left your lips
& when it left your lips
turned blue &
the mannequin at the front of science class
with its blue, detachable liver

my heart in high school was constantly
popping out it was ok it was
plastic anyway & Rhonda
the bruise above your right eye
was the center of a blue storm
I wanted to walk through & would have
I'm sorry I walked up to you & tried to lick it

11/3/2004

I cut out the eyes of a politician.
They were blue eyes. The pupils, blown wide.
& over my own eyes
I glued them, thinking, Now I can see
how utterly weak I am. Yes,
weakness spread thickly—numbingly—
to every nerve, every nerve ending.
I thought: Any second my own dog,
my ancient, bald dog
will rise & urinate on my foot. Any second
you will walk into the room
& hurl my well-hidden Box of Weakness
against my chest. You will grab
The Weakness between my legs
& order me to assume
a certain weak position . . . I will crawl,
on my hands & knees, out into the weak-feeling air,
air so weak I can hardly breathe it, out
onto the weakly-lit street
where a measly, flea-infested sparrow
will land on my head
&, as if someone pulled a string, shit
down the side of my cheek. Weeping
bird shit will surely be my weakest moment.
But because I am unable to defend myself
from this act of violence, because
I am profoundly, intensely weak,

I will perform the weakest possible act:
I will sit down in the middle of an intersection,
an intersection full of large, idling cars
& crisp, powerful pedestrians,
pedestrians freshly emerged
from vacuum-packed canisters,
& pour gasoline over my head,
& gaze up at the clean white object of a gathering cloud.

HOVE INTO VIEW

Come back here—zzt, zzt—you have my
stem cells, you have my fluids,
chemical & otherwise, exchange & movement of,
love . . . blue sparks
a blue waterfall falling
between us: something soldered,
soldered open: laughter
a series of tunnels
along our temples
a green green lawn ripples & bucks
beneath our feet O
we were shining shining
in the chemotherapeutical
afternoon. Selah.
We're still alive.
Selah. We're chewing.
We're taking things in.
We're moving at the speed of goats
over the lush & rioting landscape
leaving a desert in our wake
& pieces of our underwear
& lovemaking
& a few placental sacs,
partially nibbled. Hard to stomach
with one stomach. A goat has five.
Between us, six, & the sixth
is always empty

to remind us
we're alive: a syllable, churned
& eaten clean
until its interior—zzt, not quite—
shines through: chrome horses
riding without eyes into the mouth of a sun.

LOOPHOLE

Into the engine
he typed the words

& then the words
the words he typed

began their search
for the words

searching inside
the engine

of a man typing
with a tendon

recently torn from
a dream in which

the wet, black muzzle
of a doe behind him

spoke the words
Jean-François Revel

IF YOUR HANDS ARE TRANSPARENT, WAVE HARDER

My body aches. *Achtung!*
A letter blows across the sky.
Then nothing, not even a zephyr.
P is in Pittsburgh. He has
einen goldenen anus, like the sun,
& this wound in my left armpit shines
when I think of him. Of gewgaws
& other folderol
I will not write. My plan's
airtight: if the cabin pressure
drops below sea level
a blonde light
will leak from the gills
of a black minnow
swimming
in a clear plastic bag
on my lap. Put
the seat back. Relax.
Our sound suppressor is
packed with anemones. O
I am a solitary polyp
whose form, bright & varied colors,
& cluster of tentacles
superficially resemble
a flower. Petal
a man with epaulets &

his chest becomes a cream puff.
The sequel to sepal? In theaters
everywhere in a theater
called Spring. & still in Africa
a gnu lumbers, awkwardly,
towards me, as if starving,
as if he has something to tell me
—i.e. he moves with purpose, like
a thought, newly antlered, deciduous.

HOUR

                        a chrome hubcap
flew off
your face suddenly naked
I wish I were
similarly flat-chested as a

board my father used
a pine board to whack
a horse over the head I
couldn't believe it
bit his tit

it made a sickening
a soft sickening out of
my ears flat back as the grass

I often stick a stick
I mean I
use a pencil as a
bit my
tongue kind of likes it

O we have steered ourselves
into a
loudspeaker calling all
gear scrubbers
attention

calling all
gear scrubbers
to the factory

cordoned off by a
chainlink fence we can
put our tongues through it
I said and our
ten fingers I said
this is the Dream
of the Invisible Guillotine

it was your
horse-nostrils   America
that always jolted us awake

UNWRITTEN POEMS

One was tied to a fence post, bawling.
Another was little more than a smudge
left behind by a forehead resting
on a pane of glass. A third
was traumatized, during childhood,
by a water pick, while another formed
a deepening fetish for the rudders
of submarines. One had a bloodshot eye,
one eyelash left, while another poem
was a cell phone, hurled into a toilet.
One poem was arrested for excessive
public prayer; another,
excessive pubic hair. One
fell in love with the word "prong."
One was a necklace of living bees.
One moved like a grasshopper
trying to outrun a lawnmower.
Another bushwhacked in the nerve-factory.
One spent the entire poem holding,
out of boredom, a socket wrench
up to its eye socket, while another
argued vision is a kind of invisible
suction action. This particular poem was unable
to pull its eyes away from the TV.
This poem had a round, golf-ball-sized hole
in the back of its head. This poem the light
shining, when it sleeps face down, from that hole.

SYSTEM OF OBJECTS

Earthlyly the earth. Ovipositors
descend, lowered
by tensile cables
& deposit clouds—silken,
globular—into our mouths.
Lids open—skyward—with the lips.
We are neighborless & seamless.
We are end to end
lying in an ever-expanding
warehouse, halfway house, book.
& the red-tipped, semiautomatic sounds
of construction strafe the background, become
a jackhammer, unmanned, the ears
a pair of tunnels curving away
& into you, a maze only in this life
a blindness. Even my cat
simply by moving
parts the air. Moles measure
space by the agitation
of their whiskers. How many times
have you tried to fit.
Among the Whiskered Ones.
Among the Meek. Among the Ranks
of Lesser Clouds—this breath—
we can breathe on each other's fingers
& maybe, if I'm feeling robust, you can
jam them under my armpits

for warmth. Rubber cement.
Rubber cement. Rilke once said
I forget. Reading with earplugs:
redundant. We are already
in a soundproof studio
& I'm content to let
a swarm of silver minnows
nibble each string
of a banjo
into a smile. It's a miracle:
I'm smiling too. A bookcase,
viewed from behind, is not
the back of anyone's brains.

URBAN ANARCHISTS

We were turned on
by her offscreen

prescience: with
an iris cast

in blue steel
she smashed

the windshields
of SUVs. A crack

ran up the sky.
Abdeslam the parachutist

arrived, swinging
through it, swinging

in from a long dawn
named The Screening

of a City
Without a Future,

named The City of
Diminishing Infants

or The City of
Inverse Surveillance.

A pigeon flew
through the flames.

The look of terror
in its smoking

red eye was
my own face there

reflected.
It had begun.

There was a signal.
The signal had no name.

It was a crack in the sky.
We waited for instructions.

We put our lips inside.
Hair grew over our mouths.

Our thoughts
were white & empty

as parachutes
without chutists,

just thought balloons,
word balloons, white space,

negative space, a dialogue
was in place. We pushed off

on a giant billboard
& floated downstream.

Night fell. Nothing
replaced it. Abdeslam

started a fire
in the nostril

of Tom Hanks.
Then the pigeon

extended its
right leg, a pink twig

with a tiny,
barrel-shaped

capsule tied
to its ankle:

"Follow the river
North, through

the White Plains,
then head South.

When you reach
the scarlet beach

teeming with
flamingos

stop. I'll be
burning

further instructions
in the wings."

UNATTENDED VEHICLES RISK TOWING

Phrenologically speaking, I'm
an airhead. Preemies
are fed for the first few months
through a vein
in the head. I'm up to my gills
& face down
in the mud-covered mud. Hark!
A marsh hawk. Lightning
slakes between the bars
of my crib. You my
mobile, turning, throwing shadows,
strung with mirrors, duck bills, errors.
Everyone once
should have the pleasure of thundering
land ho! Everyone no longer
a crow's nest but a cluster of nests,
urban, suburban, some with turbans
& otherness orphans a pair of tender wings
in my cheeks. A hackysack lands in my coffee.
An old man, retired, seated next to me,
giggles. This is his corner. His bench.
Maggie just called. Her brain has
more shapes than a puzzle
composing an image of
her laughter, which fits.
The man, the retired man, is watching me.
It wasn't my grandmother

who made me flinch
but the eerie skinlessness
of her fingertips, smooth
as a turtle's neck
when touched, if touched.
The man has an unusually large head,
but only in the back, where his memories are,
I think, & stand up. Hold on there
son, he says, don't I know you
from somewhere? Pause. Then a tiny,
transparent, infinitely thin sword
slashes, in rapid, forward motions,
to the very front of my brain.

NEVER THOUGHT LOSSLY THIS WORLD & TILTING

I never thought my hands, & when I did
they were sealed tightly
inside latex. My face, when I brushed it,
felt dusted with milkweed, white parachutes
undusting a sanitized sky
white as the fluid leaking from split pods.
I often feel like a pod. Self-contained.
Detachable. Which is only the illusion
I know of safety. Stem cells
gathered around my bare, white feet.
I was standing in water, in a ditch. They seemed hungry
for something I could never give them,
names, or certain histories
that would go unnamed, discarded
along the sides of empty roads, an infant,
a tin can, a hitchhiker
stepping into view & waiting
without lifting
any of his hands.

CANCIÓN

The angle at which
she faces the sun

is not right. Her
blue forehead leaks

in the shade of the
olive tree, a slow

aerosol thought
that leaves the shape

of a heart
on bark. Dogs

the bodies of dogs
& limp,

black tire tubing
deflated, the late afternoon

haze, its airless
dry speech a thermometer

records with a thin
red throat. The typewriter

is so hot its metal keys burn
the fingertips, its

44 hammers nearly worn
to a blank alphabet. Only

the question mark remains
intact.

Black starlings
unwind a fig tree

& ribbon stage right.
Someone, earlier,

was reading Lorca
into a cool, empty well

& recording it. She
thinks of Lorca's

lost grave, the small bones
that must, by now,

remain. She thinks of
his teeth in the earth.

Molars worn down to
a few white stones,

a few imprints, or one.
She thinks about this mark.

No sound. Evening
then dusk then the night

like a series of curtains,
heavy, velvet, descends.

No stars. Over & over
she shakes the letters of his name

in her head as if her head
were a hand,

a huge, closed hand,
a fist.

CANDY STRIPERS SERVE CACTI & CANDYTUFT SALAD

to a ward of fainting goats. I
am on eo fthem. I'm typing
faster than this machine can type
because the machine itself
is dangerous. No pause
possible, especially since a bar
of space exists—infinite—
between lips. Hi Jen Hyde
you have so many sides
to your personality I need
quadrilateral glasses
equipped with night vision
to see you equidistantly emerge
between curtains, velvet, polishing
a miniature, silver pistol,
rubbing out stars
with the idea of stars
& breathing. Who says a song.
Over. Who utters
the phrase transparent gutter
& stands back as a tube of rain
slides horizontally
across the sky
with nowhere to go but
clouds, one by one

out of nowhere, throats.
Has the soil. & a hackberry
prepares tiny, beak-sized orange meals
for the birds. Between
a peduncle &
the cirri's pompous, feathered hats
a barnacle; I live
on the side of a thimble-sized
ship. No need of a dry dock.
No need of a dock. Soon
they will sell saliva. Soon
the Mouth Breathers Association
will celebrate this victory! Soon
our foreheads will pivot into this world
installed with a one inch dormer window
& we'll leave ours open
to the snow—let a flake drift in
& land, exactly, on the thought of melting,
the word *melting*—islands
floating into &, axons & end rhymes,
written ti

NOT YET BY LIGHTNING

Whatever cloud—however charged—
& loud with yellow fingers
was in your brain. There were two clouds.
Consciousness

not yet struck by an I
wants to know, wants upon waking
a face, something to face,
a window & reflection's window
into spruce trees, snow-covered

or green, forever green as long
as a red cardinal, descending
the way birds descend
in trees, limb by limb
& lightly, a controlled fall

upon waking—it was raining. Lovingly
no one's hands, imaginary, undressed you
but your own, & the limbs
mirrored knew what you knew:

they belong only to the genderlessness
of birds, how each puts on one side
of the same air & hinges upwards. I
can't even say I am, when I am,
with you, since reading

begins in gaze & a gaze never
your own in a book, its pages.
One page is never turned
but over. There were two pages.
Syllable a word in you a self
with three syllables: wordlessly,

surrender. A red dot. A low harm
in the trees. A falling art
or the art of following without need
of knowing what may, given distance,
break into wakefulness, its endless addresses
to which we, reading, barely return.

HOUR

I can believe in your hours, held
as they are hands
waving behind glass; a watch for example
is a window on the underside of a wrist
where tendons can be seen to retract
such fingers of sunlight
into a fist. I was hit by you,
and I liked it. Stupidly
the sun punches morning
after morning
through the night sky. Dust sifts down,
coating our eyelids. We wake coughing
in the post-conflict recovery tent
and kiss, crumpling our white dust masks,
threads of fiberglass in our lips.
They have invented this machine to extract
glass from the lips of strangers
which is precisely what we are,
although the fear of breathing
brings us within inches
of each other's face. This is where
you want me, so close
as to be slightly out of focus,
a single eye, four lungs,
the air between us
at rest, a rest, sweet pause
to keep our tongues from drying out.
They did dry out, but slowly, since the word
for this is never far from our lips.

HOUR

The hole was not aware it was a hole
until it was uncovered. Then it became

a manhole, which I fell through,
over & over. I tried to move the hole

but there was another hole
beneath it, which I fell through,

over & over, an O. This
was my blowhole. I breathed through it.

I took the hole inside my hole
& became the space I fell through.

Sunlight, when I opened my mouth to laugh,
leaked out of my throat. A crow

leapt from a branch
& curved into my sternum—exiting,

seconds later, behind my thigh. The crown
of my head slid open to receive the sky.

I was filled with holes. I was falling.
I tried to form a word but it was only a long,

endless moan, a moan with no bottom,
a sound I'd never heard before, rising up

from the ground: the moon rose,
& it was pocked with holes, & the stars

opened, one by one, the roof of the sky,
& I was making this sound—I couldn't stop—

it had nothing to do with me, it was holed up
inside me, I was just a rim, or a hole without a rim,

which isn't a hole at all but   this,
I thought, is a thought I can fall through, & it stuck.

O

I am no doubt not the only one who writes
in order to have no face.

Michel Foucault

THREAT ADVISORY: ELEVATED

My life vest
is lined

with the feathers
of hummingbirds

& suicides. I'm
under orders

signed by the
word order

& with no fuse
as green as

this vibration
to withhold. Pass,

heart. You're
an atrium

made to last
as long as this.

As long as this
house I say

holds up
the writing

on my throat
to light.

Flowers mouth
the word

flower. Hands
hold hands.

Even this vest
is a vestibule

for flashbacks
& therapy. A

picture of
everyone I love

burns a hole
into this

photograph.
Delayed flash.

Keep smiling.
This bus stops

for anyone
in the air.

Word is
no one self

to help
but the one

we leave
behind.

Word is
we're gathered

here together
& it's enough.

A fine speech
said Fiona.

Peerless said
Pierce. Only Mungo

looked dismayed
& so we

made love to him,
hovering,

in the old style,
a style

so old he
barely noticed.

LET CHANGE TRANSFUSE ALL OTHER TRAITS

Some pores open only to accept electronic rain
& in the end, defects litter the lawn
like plane wreckage, smoking a little
with the histories of evening skies.
I'd like to swallow a piano & kiss you
with no lips, banging our teeth
right down to the bones what music
isn't best but broken, somewhere,
along the auditory spine. We
must not wait for the sand machine
to make sand, the wave machine to make
waves, mechanical seagulls colliding
repeatedly in midair above our heads
& the sun malfunctioned & never set
so we got fried, our pores sweating beer cans
& even the horseshoe crabs maneuvering
their tanks in & out of the waves
seemed to avoid us. The idea of a snack bar
withdrew over the waves all the way to the
horizon, where it stopped, & crouched down,
waiting—we swam out to the offshore oil rig
& frolicked under its huge platform, touching
its giant pylons in the cool shade & with the soothing,
underwater sound of mechanical pumping
we made love in the heavy water, the lifeless water,
the kind of water we could smear on each other's faces
& in smearing, laugh, & in laughing, drown, & in drowning
steal beneath the skins of larger, more liquid machines.

CLOACAL DIALOGUE

Cloacal dialogue. Speech
precisely the size of the letter o
bubbles at night
from the anuses (ani?)
of fish. The structure of
patience. Dispersal. Dolphin.
A thin fin. Infinite. Nothing's
left alive behind such glass or ash
& therefore we left the aquarium
only to be carried once again
beneath rivers—what hands,
here, built that, removal of,
lit a gas lamp, earth,
hand me that rag, careful,
now a beach, disappearing—& with the air
like an enormous, invisible dog
pushing to exit the subway ahead of us
we're dispersed in a city of glass,
of skyscrapers, faces
swimming in circles, reflected
as circles, transparent, air now
rushing to fill the word
sky. A pigeon lands (of course).
Its eyes, bifurcated, panoramic,
are not bothered by its own
infinite reflection extending
between the mirrored glass skins

of buildings
& then it shits a brief white streak
& lifts into a windshield's
rotating reflections O
there is a noise
on the side of your cheek
that was once hard-wired
in the mind
of a satellite—
I don't have a set theory.
Unsettled spectacles. Bubbles.
Wings the moment they unfold
repeated, still repeating
through the face
of a man standing
with his head against the glass,
staring out
at a woman who loses her glasses
beneath the permanently hubcapless tire
of a yellow cab. How quickly
without a sense of depth, binocular,
she understands form &
walks straight
into the rising sun's oncoming highway.
Good luck lady!

DEBOUCHMENT AS A FORM OF STEREOGNOSIS

& each of us as orphans, factory-made & approved
by the soft blossoms
of aerial warfare
sang beautifully on the windowsill-sized stage.
I wanted to kneel & wash their tiny, soiled hands
until a crimson light, pink & flickering, shone
between their eyes, from their eyes, health.
But the rules of the asylum strictly prohibited
any gesture, however loving, that might lead
to inscription. Birds began to land
at the exact speed my mind wandered. He'd
been making a video of himself typing
as a way to make what he was typing
real. The soft blossoms, for instance,
are only soft if seen from the prerecorded distance
of the evening news. & then the seed
on the windowsill disappeared
& with it, the birds, save for one
who kept returning, desperate, convinced
a small grain of blonde millet remained.
At least the bird's brain was focused
on something, something precisely the size of its brain.
He closed his own eyes. He gave it a try. It was a vague,
gelatinous shape, like a milk-eyed infant king, or
    a huge collapsed pore

but that was as far as his lens would zoom.

I pulled back
my forehead from the glass. A vent at my ankle
automatically adjusted the temperature of my ankle. Outside,
on the grounds, they seemed—twirling around with their
    red, open throats—
to nearly prevent each flake from touching ground.

MEMOIR OF AN AMNESIAC

They felt the back of my neck
for a price tag. It was in my mouth.
It was under my tongue
& cutting into
the cord
keeping it from leaping
out of its cage. All seventy
macaque monkeys
hurled themselves
against the one-way glass. It bulged
outward, into a giant eyeball, & stared at us,
blinking. "I'm sorry, I thought you were . . ."
& I was. Voices
grunted in the radiator; December
stepped out of a cab
& into January, which sped off.
I was holding my stuffed animal
up to the mirror. Ducks
are vain, especially mallards,
that's why they go blind
& die there, nibbling on the end
of a shotgun. The shirt
you lent me chafed my nipples
& for the first time in 30 years
I understood the importance of undergarments.
When I was three I was attacked

by swans: Early Mythic Experience.
When I was four it was a nest of Italian bees
(honey gives me the hives). At five
a Toggenburg head-butted me
through the fence; I dropped faster
than my apple dropped—his intention.
At six I vanished for 30 seconds
into a swarm of locusts
& emerged, when they flew off,
naked & astonishingly clean. Later,
my father, a religious man, put Red Dye #5
in the hot water tank; instantly
I'd lost my mother although at eight she was replaced
by a cat who liked to lick
the salt off
my armpits & therefore accelerated my entrance
into puberty—out of the ashes, a red glow—
already he was dusted with a grape-flavored softness,
especially late, when the light burned
from such a distance that it seemed
to seep up from the ground, like sewage.
That part of the lawn stayed green until December.

HOUR

A face altered by a gust of wind
the way a cloud drifts apart into clouds,
wet with emotional sun, flakes of cum,
precisely individual pores & if pores,
a breathing face, almost out of breath.
A dream had been in place. It had stitched
his face to another's face & when he woke
he tore through the house in search of the sound
of a stone dropped inside a cistern,
how his mind became the space that echoed up
when it landed. He kept a pile of stones
in his head for this purpose. He shifted
them around. A stone inside a hole puts an end
to certain histories. His mouth was a hole.
He put a stone there. Moss grew around his lips.
He thought of the year 1671. It did nothing for him.

EVOLUTION OF BODIES INTO UPRIGHT, ADJUSTABLE LIGHTS

Love the jodhpurs. Love the hair.
A fly lands on a flyswatter
& clicks
into position. Hut one.
Hut two. Nobody move
until the day snaps
& we are roaring
in our helmets together
in mass numbers a stadium
offers the illusion of safety
unlike the fly, whose
black, robotic parts
swivel with the mechanical joy
of insects
& air, I will share it with you,
breathing, sneezing. Hence cities socialize
all things that travel in packs:
pigeons, roaches, emotions, words
we insert in meters
to pass the time between words, anyways
ants never pass without fondling
each other's faces. They have
black, reflective cheeks. My
hand is a hand puppet.
Hallowed by thy frame. Sign says
the isthmus is this way:

a string of saliva
between lips, gleaming
in klieg light, our set secured
by flamingos, birds unfolding into flames,
I could cup my hands in this wind, we
could put our liquid necks together,
who first looked up at the stars,
who first looked between the stars
& felt at home, & placed a hand, lovingly,
on the feathered back of an aging, loyal ostrich.

LUNGS OF MY INFLATABLE LIFE

unite! in the cold
a white pitcher

my blue lips
pour into shape.

A cat purrs pebbles.
A cat named Creek Bed.

A cat with emeralds
for eyes, a facet

for every surface
in the dark. Before

the snowstorm
we placed on the grass

a photograph of
the sun. Over time

a word. Over time
paint

chipped & the angels
slowly revealed

in the moment of
their arrival

on the wall
looked astonished.

We were born
with two wings

& only on the inhale
is this given air

divided. For warmth
I stare at the snow.

Remember to breathe
was never anyone's

last words. Each crystal
Wayne is shining

from more surfaces
than my eyes

can stand. This must be
infinity. This

must be why it took me
three years

to figure out my cat
is blind.

GLENN GOULD'S CHAIR

It was a miniature chair.
It was a wooden chair.
He brought it with him
everywhere. Some say
it allowed him to remain
a child, reaching up
to the high white keys.
Or that his fingers moved
more freely once freed
by the weight of his arms.
Year after year he played
on the chair. When the
upholstery fell apart
he sat on the wooden slats.
In certain recordings
one can hear it creaking.
It was keeping time. It was
a piece of time. He sat
on time & eternity
was the endless variations
of tiny hammers kissing
a string—a line—drawn through
the ears of the ears of the audience,
through the microphones,
the speakers, these headphones.
& when he finished he stood up
& folded the chair. These are the most complex

of all chairs: they are mostly
air. He knew music would be nothing
without air & this is why
one can hear him breathing
—grunting—behind the music.
He was making sure it was there.
Some even argue he sat in such a way
that his ass, while playing,
never *actually* touched the chair . . .

HOMELESS CLONE

Do you read me, copy? Are you
like me defenestrated
by images of broken windows? I live
on a street with no sign,
no sidewalk, no swan-necked
street lamps to light the addresses.
My only homing device: a wingless pigeon.
He leads me beside the still waters of
the BQE. I say Harold how did you lose
your wings but he doesn't answer.
I say Harold the evening sky darkens,
the buildings seem unfamiliar,
there are no lights in the long windows,
why these silent tanks
waiting at the far ends of the alleyways.
He doesn't answer. He is almost lost
in the night ahead of me, a small shadow
on the concrete, flitting
around corners, a tiny speck of gray
disappearing down wide, empty streets,
I can barely see his cuneiform, forking
bird-prints, illegible in the dust,
turning into doorways, into courtyards, rooms.
It is so dark I am afraid to move. I
feel something soft brush my face,
something moving gracefully, tracing
a pattern, a series of rings, a helix

in the air around me, invisible. Harold
I call out softly, Harold . . .
He doesn't answer. He never answers.

HOUR OF SECRET AGENTS

The code word, he whispered, just before
letting go, was code word. Asshole,
I thought, watching his head
get smaller and smaller until it ended
in a puff of dust. Where it began,
I thought again, and spun around.
The landfill stretched on for miles.
I heard the voices of lost products beneath me.
My wheelbarrow was missing a wheel. A red bird
flew by, as if on a mission to flee this landscape
as soon as possible. The charred body of an infant
crawled out from a plastic bag. I stepped back,
covering my mouth. It crawled
a little further, then collapsed.
A pre-recorded voice announced it was feeding time.
I masticated my last handful of brazil nuts
but it took forever; by the time I finished
I'd forgotten what I was doing and swallowed.
Nobody wanted you anyway, I shouted,
when it began to cry. My wheelbarrow
was missing a wheel. I'll never get out of here.
It was just a barrow. I flipped it over
on top of the infant. "Ancient graves,"
I wrote in my notebook, "are where the living
feel most alive." A bulldozer
started up, two mounds over. Seagulls
swarmed its yellow bucket raising

piles of blue surgical gowns
to the sun. The skin on my face tightened.
The bird with the red breast flew by again
precisely in the same direction, which confused me.
The rubber soles of my shoes were burning.
Coils of smoke rose between fissures.
From the tip of a far-off mound
a CD repositioned the sun
straight into my eyes, although it could have been
a signal, the permission I was waiting for,
the sign I was clear to return, was once again
unknown, or no longer known, a night sky,
the honesty of stars, a bowl of glass oranges
centered on a table, centered in a room,
a room that had never been opened
or if it had, by a trembling, white glove.
The infant was still crying in its makeshift grave.
The red bird flew by again, this time in my mind.

INSOMNIA

I don't remain awake.
It does. I observe it.
It observes me. Together
we see a Queen's
sea-blackened teeth
or a satellite view
of a dying coral reef.
This skeleton's arranged
in an X. Next attempt:
a helix. Dust
I would say you
drift within a city
the future holds
upon landing, city
of runaways where
all stars are the lights
of airplanes, waiting
to land, where a face,
its faceness, circles you
in a room, blinking,
hello, I am human, these
are my cheeks, their bones,
beneath which are the wires
& pockets of white sand
& a blown-glass planet
& the single leaf
I placed inside it, suspended,

green—a veined hand, waving.
Never will I recall
its name. A blue jay
muscles its way
through a tree. Birds
sew the eyes
into such bright seeds.
Smile wide the sky.
I lean on sunlight
as on a strange, invisible cane.

ALIEN CORN

Here a field
I feel

folded into me
with green

before I see it
wave, as a

wave, over me.
Some days it

knocks my
fake beard off

my ears
with the word

"codpiece." Disguise
she said

is the machine's
first function.

Then she removed
her Donald Duck

mask &
lay with me,

down, in the
field from which

my mind was waving
to her.

Only later did I
notice her

ears. They were
the ears of an

alien. & still
I spoke

knowing their
long white silk

was also part
of the machine,

as is my hand,
waving,

a gesture as simple
as hello, are

we too far
gone

in this field
to hear its leaving

KEEP ME INFORMED OF YOUR PROGRESS

For you will I
turn on

my electronic
voice scrambler.

This shadow-cloud
of shifting pixels

only follows a face
in speech. That's

my ear there
in the upper left

square: my eyes,
overlapping. If I

gaze upon my throat
in the mirror

it's only to remember
I have an interior

life. Once I
lowered a camera down

an abandoned well
& waited for the

timed flash. Each
of us a secret

a hand or a scan
or a surgical cam

can't reach. The
writing on the inside

of these walls becomes
the walls, becomes

a dog
for example

with the letters
a black dog

is barking
at its shade or

shadow, at the
echo of his own bark

in the mountains,
the simulation

of a dog or mountain
occurs, a book.

The flash never
went off; into

this book I pasted
the walls & the echo

of the color black.
Whatever light

was a sound. I
listened to it

in the mirror.
Approaching "a"

or a secret or what's
unspoken there

in our reflection
one's voice

takes on the rising
metallic whine

only found in the
history of insects,

a cicada. Here
they are everywhere

in the trees unwinding
their eyes into the

light. That
was a deep image

although it did not rise
from a shallow place

since their eyes
are blind & stupid

& full of advertising.
Today someone announced

he was Deep Throat.
I think about his voice.

When he made those calls.
Its clarity.

ANOLES CHOOSE THE BACKGROUND INTO WHICH THEY DISAPPEAR

All's well
in my house

of cards.
The Queen's

black eye—
my window

outside. I
see a finch

in the grass
having an

asthma attack.
All hands

on deck!
I breathe

using only
the Designated

Breathing Machine
which is shaped

like the body
of a boneless

swan. A mole
below me

sneezes—two
quick shrieks.

Furious red
objects unfurl

from the mouth
of the dog

next door.
On this desert

floor I can
even hear

what we once
called the sea,

how we sang by it
thinking

we were geniuses.
Splash splash.

No more immersion.
The frogs with

double heads
are harmonizing

with themselves,
are calling . . .

HOUR

I mark the spot.
I make an incision.
On the exhale
I make an incision.
The hand is mine
that marks the spot
that makes the incision
on the exhale—slowly—
in the folds.
In this way I fold
myself inside
the folds, cutting deeper.
A noxious odor escapes.
My goggles fog.
I was afraid
I might wake you
although you're watching
me awake: an apple
hangs muted
by the beauty
in which it hangs
among the other apples
wrinkled by thoughts
frozen in the ground
of autumn. I mark
the spot. I make
an incision.

A yellow bird escapes
& clamps its beak
on the end of my chin.
I can't shake it off.
A partially chewed
action figure
climbs up my sleeve.
My lips tremble.
I throw them away.
& behind my lips
an orchard wilts.
I say orchard
& the orchard
wilts. I say wilt
& Thou arrives
with tiny bird cages
swinging from his eyes.
This is how it was
packaged. This
is why I cut into it &
suctioned the clouds
out of the sky & the
three black crows
that thought they
owned it, which is
part of their packaging.
In order to be opened

exhale completely
smooth your lungs
into a bright cloth
& cast it
into the winter
of a long sewing.
This will almost
be enough.

THE ENTERPRISE

The hatch opens, read the instructions,
only in one direction: into you. Instantly
I pulled my hand away
from the handle
while a voice, my own,
but deeper—movie-trailer deep—spoke the words:
He's pulling his hand away from the handle.

The hatch was a glass hatch, six inches thick.
I could see the magnificent blue marble
of the earth, which bored me.
Even if it looked like an enormous eyeball floating in space
it would still bore me. An asteroid
rotating like an asteroid—that is, slowly—
passed by. I thought:
perhaps this isn't a hatch
after all, but the glass surface of a game, a video game . . .

Certain electric typewriters
have a silver, round typing ball, circled
with letters, symbols, punctuation, all slightly raised. When
      you hit a key . . .
& the first telegraph, invented in Spain, involved 26
      humans, each
holding the end of a wire. When a letter
was struck in the next town, sending an electric current
down the wires, the corresponding human, once electrocuted,

screamed its assigned letter.
The earth returned, this time
even smaller. A thin script of clouds
began to form, increasingly dense,
swirling inward, or rings swirling outward,
unwinding from some furious, endlessly regenerating center
or into it, I couldn't tell.

Nervously I squeezed food from a syringe
directly into my mouth. This,
despite the warning label:
Insert Only Into Abdominal Feeding Tube.
My mouth, at some level, is still a feeding tube.
Also, conceivably, my ears, my ear canals. Perhaps
the first instructions were not written down,
or out. Perhaps they weren't even spoken.

The earth, by now, was nearly invisible, gone.

Acknowledgments

Thanks to John Ashbery a chapbook-length selection of these poems first appeared in a special issue of *Conjunctions* titled "Beyond Arcadia: New Young American Poets"; thanks to Kate Hall and Heather Jessup, editors of Delirium Press, a chapbook called *HourHour*, with drawings by the artist Ryan Mrozowski, was published in 2005; and thanks to Gregor Podlogar a number of these poems were translated into Slovenian for *Dnevi poezije in vina*, 2006. I want to acknowledge, with gratitude, the following editors whose persistence allowed many of these poems to appear in magazines: Susan Denning *(Caffeine Destiny)*; Josh Kotin *(Chicago Review)*; Annabelle Yeeseul Yoo and Frances Justine Post *(Columbia: A Journal of Literature and Art)*; Amber Curtis, Amy Schrader, and Joshua Marie Wilkinson *(Cranky)*; Brett Lauer and Aimee Kelley *(CROWD)*; Joshua Marie Wilkinson and Danielle Dutton *(Denver Quarterly)*; Justin Lacour *(Kulture Vulture)*; Dara Cerv and Kathleen Rooney *(Redivider)*; and Brenda Shaughnessy *(Tin House)*. "The Performing Understanding" re-frames works by Ana Mendieta and Vito Acconci. Finally, to the first citizens, Cort Day, Matthew Zapruder, and Lori Shine: thank you.